GOL
YOU

BRUCE VAN NATTA

Edited by Frank A. DeCenso Jr.

DESTINY IMAGE PUBLISHERS

Scripture is the authors' own. Please note that Destiny Image's publishing style capitalizes certain pronouns in Scripture that refer to the Father, Son, and Holy Spirit, and may differ from some publishers' styles. Take note that the name satan and related names are not capitalized. We choose not to acknowledge him, even to the point of violating grammatical rules.

DESTINY IMAGE® PUBLISHERS, INC.
P.O. Box 310, Shippensburg, PA 17257-0310

"Speaking to the Purposes of God for this Generation and for the Generations to Come."

This book and all other Destiny Image, Revival Press, Mercy Place, Fresh Bread, Destiny Image Fiction, and Treasure House books are available at Christian bookstores and distributors worldwide.

For a U.S. bookstore nearest you, call 1-800-722-6774.

For more information on international availability, call 717-532-3040.

Reach us on the Internet at www.destinyimage.com.

Digital Edition ISBN: 978-0-7684-1854-5

Trade Paper ISBN: 978-0-7684-1853-8

Originally published in *Hearing and Understanding the Voice of God*, ISBN 978-0-7684-3803-1.

GOD WILL TALK THROUGH YOU

BRUCE VAN NATTA

GOD WILL TALK THROUGH YOU

When I began writing this, I had already written a whole book on hearing God's voice, but I didn't want to base this on just my "old" material. I began to pray for the Lord to give me some "fresh" revelation knowledge that I could share with you, those hungry to hear from God, but wasn't getting anything. One day, I shut myself up in my bedroom and climbed on top of our bed with a notebook and pen and told the Lord I wasn't going to move until

He spoke something. I prayed for quite awhile with not much happening and have to admit I started to get sleepy. At the point I was about to fall asleep the Lord gave me a very simple vision.

It was a vision of a large "ear" of corn. The husk was still on it but had been pulled back in one spot to reveal the golden kernels of ripe corn underneath. It vanished, and I asked the Lord what it meant. Then the Holy Spirit spoke and said, "He who has *ears* let him hear" (see Matt. 13:9). I chuckled at God's sense of humor and obvious use of a pun, but had to admit to Him that I didn't understand what He was saying! The Holy Spirit spoke again and told me that when we hear *and* understand His "word" we will produce a crop and then told me to go to the parable of the four soils and He would show me something I hadn't seen before. Much of the following chapter is based on what He began to show me about a parable that I always thought was only to do with salvation.

In Matthew chapter 13, Mark chapter 4, and Luke chapter 8, Jesus tells the parable of the four soils and then gives His disciples the meaning of it. If we study all four accounts, we can get a clearer picture of what Jesus is saying.

He talks about a farmer who went out to sow his seed. As he did, some fell on the path and was eaten by the birds.

Some seed fell on rocky ground where it sprang up quickly, but ended up withering because it had no root. Some seed fell among thorns, which grew and choked the plants, and some seed fell on good soil where it produced a crop a hundred, sixty, or thirty times what was sown.

Jesus tells us in Luke 8:11 that the seed is the "Word" of God. The Greek word for *Word* here is *Logos*. According to the Strong's concordance, this is a spoken or written communication with a focus on the content (often about who God is or what He is like). He goes on to explain that the four types of soil represent the four ways that people can respond to the "word," or again some type of communication from God including who He is and what He is like.

We learn that the first group is those who hear about God or from God but don't understand. They, therefore, don't believe and the "word" is snatched from them.

The second group is those who hear a message about the kingdom and receive it with joy, until a time of testing comes and then they fall away from the "word."

The third group of people is compiled of those who hear the "word," but are choked by life's worries, riches, and pleasures, and they do *not mature* and are *unfruitful*.

Jesus says this about the last group of people in Matthew 13:23, "...*the seed that fell on good soil is the man **who hears the word and understands it. He produces a crop,** yielding a hundred, sixty or thirty times what was sown*" (NIV). The other Gospel accounts add that this group of people not only heard the "word" and understood it, but they **accepted** it, **retained** it, and **persevered** to produce a crop.

This parable or message was so important that Jesus said that if a person didn't know or understand this parable that they wouldn't be able to know or understand *any* parable! (See Mark 4:13.)

Why was this message so important? I believe that Jesus placed such emphasis on this parable for two big reasons. It not only explains how all people can and will react to a salvation message about God, but it also defines the **principle truths** as to how a person responds to the specific messages, or individual "words" from God and what outcome that has on their life and the Kingdom! Either they will be fruitful in that particular area, or they will not.

Jesus clearly says that we need to not only **hear His voice, but to understand it** in order to produce a crop and be fruitful. Remember that when we looked at all three Gospel accounts of the parable we found that Jesus clarified this truth by saying that we would accept the "word," **retain** it, and **persevere** until we produced a crop. It is clear from Scripture that this principle truth extends to every area of our lives and therefore the Kingdom as a whole.

So if a person who fit into the first category, or way of responding, heard a salvation message, they wouldn't understand or believe it and, therefore, would not get saved. If a person from the second category heard a salvation message they would accept Jesus into their heart until something bad happened, at which point they would entirely give up on God and reject Him.

When a person from the third category hears a salvation message they accept it, but Jesus says that they never mature and remain unfruitful because of various reasons. When the people from the last category hear a salvation message, they hear and understand it—accepting it, retaining it, and persevering or abiding in Him until they produce a crop. This crop would start as their own personal salvation, but could then include countless other things such as helping to bring others to faith, showing love, working of miracles, etc.

OUR DAILY CHOICES

Let's see what the principle truths from this parable look like in our day-to-day existence as a Christian. The four groups or categories that Jesus pointed out are simply four different ways we can respond to His "words." Just because we respond one way to something He is telling us doesn't mean that we will respond that same way to another thing He tries to tell us. So even though we might be hearing, understanding, and bearing fruit in one area of our life, we can be resisting God, (either knowingly or unknowingly) in another situation and therefore be unfruitful in that region. So we could be obedient about worshiping Him regularly, but ignore Him when He tries to get us out of our comfort zone in another area, like witnessing for example. If we are honest with ourselves we can also usually think of some areas that we have resisted what the Lord was telling us because we weren't willing to change or respond. We are not always responding to Him in the same method or from the same category.

In fact, just because we have responded in a certain way to a certain "word" doesn't mean that we won't change our response at a later time. As a person goes through different seasons or phases in life, we can see how, at some point, they didn't hear or understand what the Lord was telling them in a certain area until later. For example, many believers didn't know or understand the blessings that come with tithing and giving when they were new believers, but realized its value and importance as they matured in the Lord.

The message or "word" about tithing and giving is a great one to use for an illustration as to how these principle truths from the parable apply to our daily decisions. If a believer chooses the first response type to this topic they would not understand or believe the message about tithing and that truth would be "snatched" from them. They would lose any blessings they could have gotten from following it, and would not be a blessing in that area to others either.

When a believer chooses the second response type, they would hear about tithing and begin to do it for a short time, but as soon as finances looked tight or they didn't receive some immediate benefits, they would quickly stop. There would be no fruit or crop with this choice as well.

A believer who chooses the third response type would hear about tithing and begin to do it for a season, but after they realized how much their tithe totaled over time, they would start to think about all the other things they could do with that money (a new vehicle, an exotic vacation, pay off the mortgage, more for the retirement plan, a new deck, unpaid bills, etc.) and they would talk themselves out of continuing to tithe and give regularly.

The believer who chooses the last way of responding to God's "Word" about tithing and giving would not only understand the concept, but would begin to follow this plan. They would also decide that no matter what, they were not going to stop giving back to the Lord. As the days, months, and years passed, they would remain faithful to this commitment and would begin to see a harvest or crop of blessings come back to them in many ways, just as the Lord has promised. (See 2 Corinthians 9:6-15.)

This is why it is so important to be able to **hear** what the Lord is saying to us and also be able to **understand** how we are to apply that knowledge, so that we can be blessed and be a blessing to others! Every Christian in the right frame of mind should want to be in the center of the Lord's will for their life, hearing and understanding Him so that they can lead a fruitful life.

HEARING GOD

We can't understand or even know what the Lord is saying to us unless we can hear Him. So hearing God is the first step or foundation for everything that is Kingdom minded. Sadly, there are many Christians around the world who would honestly say that they have never heard the Lord speak to them. Yet, Jesus tells us in John 8:47, *"He who belongs to God hears what God says"* (NIV). How can we explain this discrepancy?

From what I have encountered, I believe that, although there are many answers to that question, one stands out above the rest: people's expectations and assumptions as to how God speaks. Some think that God has told people all He is ever going to and that He has no perceivable interaction with his followers on a personal level any more. Then there are those who believe that if God were to speak to you it would be absolutely unmistakable, thunder and lightning would be going off, the earth would be shaking, and a loud voice would come from the sky that would penetrate you to your very core. Although God can and sometimes does speak to people this way, it is the exception, not the "norm." Often, when God speaks to us, we could easily miss it if we weren't paying attention and listening for Him.

If we were to look at every single example in the Bible of when the Lord communicated with someone, we would see that sometimes He did it directly while at other times it was indirectly. We would also find that all of these instances could be put in one of seven different categories or methods that God uses to speak to people. He meant it when He said *"I the LORD do not change"* (Mal. 3:6 NIV). He will speak to us today in the same ways He spoke to those in the Bible..

We don't want to ever try to put God in a box or limit Him by narrowly defining these broad categories, but we do want to see what He has done in the past so that we can know what to expect in the future. The following seven categories describe the ways that we can anticipate the Lord to speak to us today. **By knowing how we can expect Him to speak to us, we can better understand how to hear Him.**

1. **God talks through the process of prayer.** While this may sound very elementary, it is actually much deeper. When we pray, God hears and answers us. Although it may not always be the answer we want or expect, He will

answer and speak through His answers. We can also fully expect to hear Him in the process of praying or talking with Him, which is meant to be a two-way conversation, an exchange.

2. **God talks through the Bible.** Our Lord has given us the Bible so that we may know certain things about Him and our journey in this life. The Bible's verses are His very "words" to us, and we can fully believe that He is speaking to us through all that is written in it. As we read the Bible or even other items that contain the principles found in Scripture, we can expect to hear God speaking directly to us about our individual and specific needs, wants, or issues.

3. **God talks through the spoken Word.** God can speak to you through the preacher at church, on television, or on the radio. He can give you a message through your parent, spouse, or children. God can and will even use surprising outlets to deliver His "word" to us. The source is not important; we must remember the power is in the message not the messenger. We need to be ready to hear God speak to us whether it is through a stranger, friend, or even an enemy.

4. **God talks through the Holy Spirit.** The number of ways that the Lord can speak to us through the Holy Spirit is uncountable. It could be anything from

an audible voice to a thought, from an inner whisper to a feeling, from a perception to a physical sensation. It can be an awareness or discernment of things in the natural or spiritual realm. No matter what way the Holy Spirit speaks to us, a receptive heart can expect to hear Him day in and day out!

5. **God talks through design and circumstance.** The Bible tells us that God speaks to us through all of creation or nature, from the big things to the little things. His design carries over into even our circumstances, or what some might call fate or destiny. God is able to weave His divine plan throughout the generations despite the devil, bad choices, or

our sin. There is no such thing as coincidence, and we need to hear what God is saying even through the mundane.

6. **God talks through dreams and visions.** While not every dream or vision we have is from God, the Lord continues to communicate with us whether we are awake or asleep. Sometimes dreams are quite literal, and we will know exactly what they mean. At other times, they are more symbolic like the parables are, and we will need the Holy Spirit to interpret them. We should anticipate hearing from God through our dreams and the images that we see in our mind.

7. **God talks through angels.** The Lord is still sending His angels to this

earth. Many believers will testify to feeling their presence, while others whose spiritual eyes have been opened will actually see them. We know from Scripture that we would never worship these beings or believe anything given by one that is contrary to what we find in the Bible. They are God's servants and, even if they are silent, we can still hear God speaking to us through their presence.

When we know how we can expect our Lord to speak to us, it puts us in a position of better understanding how to hear Him. It's not even a question as to if He is speaking to us or not. The real question is, *Are we listening to Him?* Are we honestly seeking the Lord and His will for us, and are we trying to hear Him? In other words, are our hearts receptive?

After telling the parable of the four soils, Jesus quotes the Old Testament prophet Isaiah and states in Matthew 13:15 that people whose hearts have become calloused can hardly hear with their ears. He is obviously talking about a person's spiritual ears at this point. Each of us need to examine our heart and see if there are any areas in it that have become calloused and prevented us from hearing everything that the Lord is saying to us. It is rather easy to become deceived in a certain area and the danger is that we wouldn't realize it!

We can become so comfortable with a sin in our life that we don't even think it's wrong, or we can begin to believe that God just winks at that little old sin. I have met people who have continued to pray over an issue that is clearly forbidden in the Bible and then wonder why the Lord isn't granting their improper request, or blessing their sin. The Lord has given us the Scriptures and will not do, say, or bless something that is contrary to them no matter how much we pray for it.

I have seen others who have petitioned the Lord over something that is clearly explained in the Bible and then wondered why the Lord hasn't answered their question. If we claim to be a Christian, He wants and expects us to spend time in the Bible and will sometimes be quiet to force us to search the matter out in His Word.

There are also times where the Lord has spoken something to us and knows full well we have heard Him, but have not acted on what He has said. During those times, He can become seemingly silent for a time, waiting for us to respond to what He has already communicated before moving on to the next thing.

All of us need to be intentional about making ourselves open and available to what the Lord is saying. Remember

Jesus told us that we need to accept His "word," retain it, and persevere. These words describe someone who is *actively* engaged in the process. We need to be hungry for the truth and eager to hear Him and respond when He speaks to us, no matter what method He chooses to deliver His *Word*.

Understanding God

Jesus explained in our parable that we needed to not only hear but also to understand in order to produce a crop. When the Lord first gave me the vision of the ear of corn, I was hearing Him in a way, but still not understanding Him yet. It wasn't until I pressed in further that I was given more information, at which point I was able to understand what the meaning was. The choice was mine and I could have easily dismissed what I saw because I didn't understand it initially.

Jesus said that the people from the first group are those who hear from God but don't understand and, therefore, don't believe. So it is clear we have a choice whether to believe the messages that God gives. Some people will reject what the Lord says because they don't understand it. The Bible tells us not believing a message that the Lord has spoken to us can make it of no value or profit to us (see Heb. 4:2).

Unfortunately, I can think of several times in my own life where this exact thing has happened to me. Sometimes the consequences were not long lasting, while they were permanent at other times.

Several years ago, the Holy Spirit started urging me to go visit two immediate family members at their new house. Although I knew it was the Lord leading me to do this, I didn't know why. I was really struggling with some personal problems that week, so I honestly didn't want to be around anyone at the time.

The next day, the Lord again kept urging me to go over there or to at least call. Because I didn't understand why it was so important, I disregarded it and justified my actions by telling the Lord I would go when I was feeling better. That night, one of the two committed suicide. I had no idea that there were any depression issues with the person and there was nothing in the natural that would have made me even begin to think that something like that was going to happen. I didn't understand the urgency and, therefore, didn't believe that I really needed to go right then.

This is a classic example of what happens when we choose the first response type to a message from God. We hear the "word" but don't understand it and then decide not to believe it. At that point, God's message does not bless us or those it was originally intended to. I am reminded of the reality of that truth every time I see my family member who lost their spouse and how it has affected their life to this day. Thank the Lord for forgiveness when we blow it!

Many Christians would say that they will do their best to be obedient when they are certain that they have heard from the Lord about something. The problem comes when we are not completely certain if we have heard from the Lord or have heard Him correctly. It could be that the impression is brief, or that it doesn't seem to make any sense, or that the Lord is speaking in a way that we are not familiar with.

As I travel around the world ministering, much of what I do is "hands-on ministry" (and "hands-on learning" for that matter). After speaking at a place,

I will always invite people forward for prayer if given the chance, and the Lord will often speak to me about the people I am ministering to. I have learned that sometimes the Lord will tell me something that makes no sense in the natural until I begin to act on it. This might mean that I need to begin saying a certain thing or doing a certain thing even if it goes against my natural instincts. There have been times where it has felt like a test to see if I will step out on the water, but I know that the Lord uses these opportunities to prove to me that **I can trust Him even when I don't initially understand Him.** This concept is true for all believers and applies to our entire walk with the Lord!

I will never forget the first time that He gave me a *word* for someone through the use of pain. I had only been in ministry a short time and had traveled to another state to speak. During the early part of the service, my right ankle began to hurt horribly. I prayed for the Lord to take the pain away, but there was no change. The worship ended and it was now time for me to go stand up front to speak. As I began walking up the steps of the altar, I was complaining to the Lord as to why He wouldn't take the pain away, and that still, small whisper told me I didn't understand. It then dawned on me that this might be about someone else. I asked the Lord to take the pain away if it was an injury or attack from the enemy, but to allow it to remain if it was a "word" for somebody who had ankle pain.

As I stood behind the podium, it began to hurt even worse. I had never been in this church before and was told that most of the people in this denomination were a little skeptical about this whole "healing" thing. I had also never prayed for people before speaking; prayer had always come after the message in the past. But I didn't want to have to try and speak with this pain. I asked the audience whose right ankle was hurting so badly that they could barely put any weight on it. A woman right near the front stood up and said it was her. I prayed from where I was, and the Lord instantly healed her ankle and then took the pain away from me also.

Initially, I didn't understand the pain was from the Lord, but after pressing in He made it clear it was. Apparently He didn't want the woman to have to sit through the message with the pain, and, maybe even more importantly, He wanted to set the tone for a very powerful night of ministry. The Lord is speaking to us; and if we want to produce a crop, we need to believe or accept His messages, even when we don't initially understand them.

Time of Testing

Jesus tells us in our parable that the second response to a message from God is to fall away during a time of testing. It is clear from Scripture that there will be times we are tested, and often the Lord will test us concerning something that He has spoken to us just like He did with Abraham with Isaac. These tests can really vary as to what they look like, and many times we won't even recognize them as a test at first.

Maybe a person feels like the Lord has given them a certain verse or promise about an issue, but the problem gets worse instead of better. Some good examples would be Joseph or David. They both were promised positions of leadership, but both got demoted before they were eventually promoted. It was their choice, just as it is our choice if we are going to let go of what the Lord said, or hang on to it and persevere.

Sometimes the Lord will only give us a sliver of information and then expect us to respond in faith. In other words believe that we can accept what He is saying and then act on it. This is just as true for everyday life as it is for ministry. Like the vision of the ear of corn, it could be a simple picture in our mind or it could be just one word that drops in as a thought. The test at these times is, *Will we accept and persevere with what the Lord is saying when it is such a small piece of information?*

Another test this can bring up is, *Will we begin to "fill in the blanks" with our own limited knowledge instead of relying completely on the Lord?* In other words, God speaks something to us, but there aren't many details; so, we begin to try to make sense of it in the natural and add our ideas to God's "word." This is when we can "muddy the water" by making false assumptions.

Once while ministering in Toronto, Canada, I had this very thing happen. Before the service, we were praying and the Lord began to give words of knowledge about people that would be attending. He told us some names, He told us some prayer requests that people had, and then He showed me a very clear picture of the right side of a man's shiny bald head. I saw it as if I were looking down from above and the Lord said that this man's prayer would be answered. We wrote the "words" down as we drove to the church, and I described in detail to my friend the shiny bald head and the odd angle I saw it from.

After speaking that night I started calling out the words of knowledge from the list *before* opening it up for general prayer. Each item on the list was resolved, and the prayers were gloriously answered one by one until we got to the bald-headed vision. I was trying to decide how to call this one out when a man in an electric scooter came up the center aisle and didn't stop until he hit the altar. My blood ran cold as I looked down and saw the right side of his shiny bald head *and* an equally shiny **artificial leg!**

I had not called this word of knowledge out yet, so at that point, I asked the crowd if there were any other bald men in the place with a shiny head. No one else came forward, so I went out in the crowd myself looking for someone else that fit the description. When I couldn't find anybody I came back to the front and handed my partner the microphone. I told him to tell the people what the Lord had told me before the service. He shook his head no. I urged him on so I could hear with my own ears what God had said again. I knew in my spirit God could do a creative miracle and give this man a new leg, but my mind and body were struggling with the idea.

After my friend spoke out what the Lord had shown me and said that the bald man would get his prayer answered,

I handed the bald man the microphone and told him to tell everyone what his prayer request was. I looked away knowing that he was about to ask the Lord for a new leg. To my shock, he said he needed deliverance from a certain issue. At this point my faith skyrocketed. When I placed my hands on him and said a quick prayer, the power of God came on him like high voltage electricity; and everyone who saw it agreed that it looked like he had been violently electrocuted. When he woke up a while later, he told us he felt entirely better.

This had clearly been a test for me, and I almost failed it because of my wrong assumptions and fears. This world, the devil, and even our own thoughts will try to get us to doubt what the Lord tells us, but when we hang on to His "word" we can and will pass the tests.

THE THORNS

Jesus said that the third type of response to a message from God was when a person hears the "word" but life's worries, riches, and pleasures choke it, making it unfruitful and the person immature. This is when we know what the Lord has told us, but there is something else that tries to convince us to turn away or turn back from God's "word."

We might immediately think of all of the obvious sinful traps of the world that are there to draw us away from the Lord like drugs, alcohol, sexual temptations, greed, and so on, but the traps can also be more deceptive.

The devil can use "good" things to prevent us from fulfilling the "great" things that God has for us. Our good intentions are useless unless we are guided by the Lord every step of the way. Even after we have gotten a good start of hearing and understanding something from the Lord, we have the ability to throw it away if we don't persevere to the end. During the process, there is a danger we can get off track from the Lord's will if we are not diligent, continuing to abide in Him. Hebrews 12:1-2 says *"…let us throw off everything that hinders and the sin that so easily entangles, and let us run with perseverance the race marked out for us. Let us fix our eyes on Jesus, the author and perfecter of our faith"* (NIV).

I once heard a man speaking who had been setting up a large crusade in India in 2004. He had spent much money making preparations for the event and had already taken one trip over there to do some ministry and get things ready. When it came time for him to fly back to India for the crusade, the Lord told him not to get on the plane. He couldn't understand why not and reminded the Lord of the large amount of money and time already invested in the crusade. After arguing with the Lord for a while, he ended up not getting on the plane. A few days later, the horrible tsunami that took so many lives hit right in the exact area he was supposed to have held the crusade.

This man ended up making the right choice, the mature choice, but said that it was a very close decision because of the time and money already invested. I have thought about his situation more than once and wondered if I would have gotten on that plane. It is often our limited knowledge or natural type thinking that keeps us from understanding, believing, or acting on a message from the Lord. Proverbs 3:5 says it best, *"Trust in the LORD with all your heart and lean not on your own understanding*" (NIV). When we truly do this, God can protect us from all of the "thorns" that are trying to choke us and make us unfruitful and immature.

Producing a Crop

In this parable, we have seen that each of us are going to respond to the "words" or different messages that the Lord sends us in one of four ways. Jesus sums up the fourth response type in Matthew 13:23 *"...the seed that fell on good soil is the man who hears the word and understands it. He produces a crop, yielding a hundred, sixty, or thirty times what was sown"* (NIV). The proof that we have heard and understood a message from the Lord is that we accept it, retain it, and persevere until there is a crop. The crop or fruit validates this last choice.

There is a multiplication factor that exists when we are truly in the flow of what God is doing. As He multiplied the fish and loaves, He multiplies the effects of our meager efforts when we are obedient to Him and abiding in Him. As I heard someone say, He adds the super to our natural to get "supernatural" results. As He sows His seed in our hearts, and it comes to fruition, many, many, people will be touched. It becomes a chain reaction, whereby He compounds His efforts and effects through us. This is the fruit.

The great thing about this is that as long as we are alive, it is never too late to get on board with what God is doing. In the parable about the two sons, we might be like the first son who initially tells his Father "No," but ends up being obedient (see Matt. 21:28-32). This could be in regards to God in general or it could be just about a particular message or "word" that He has spoken to us. Our God is a God who restores the years eaten by the locusts when we rend our hearts and return to Him (see Joel 2).

The Lord literally called my name in a church when I was 19 to call me into ministry, but I ran from Him. After twenty years of alcohol and drugs and many bad choices, He stepped into my life and got me on a path back to Him. Shortly after that, a huge logging truck fell on top of me and basically severed my body in half. I had an out-of-body experience where I got to see the two angels that the Lord sent to save me. (Doctors say that I am the only person in the world known to have lived after having main arteries severed in my chest in five places.) During my year in and out of the hospital, and after five major operations, a documented creative miracle happened. The Lord gave me back several feet of small intestine so that I wouldn't end up starving to death, as most of my small intestine had been removed because of the accident.

After all of this, I ended up going into full-time, traveling ministry. I tell people what the Lord has done for me and for others and, more important-ly, what He will do for them. We invite people forward for prayer and then get to sit back and watch God do amaz-ing things. The Lord has shown me over and over that He wants to empower *all* believers to make an impact in this world, to produce fruit for His King-dom. At times, the Lord will have me pray for people and, after some mira-cles have happened, the Lord tells me to have those people pray for the next people who pray for the next people and so on. Each time this has happened it has been very powerful, but one time stands out because the Lord Jesus appeared to explain what was happening.

I preached in a small, denominational church that I had been told was pretty dead. After speaking, I prayed for some people, at which point the Lord instructed me to tell the last person healed that they were to pray for the next in line and so on. As the miracles continued, the people in attendance were getting more and more excited and began to crowd around the altar and loudly praise God.

I stepped back from the group when the Holy Spirit instructed me to go over to a small area that housed the piano and to go inside. As I stepped into the area, I saw Jesus sitting at a pew that had been placed between the wall and the piano. His back was to the wall and He was looking out across the piano toward the people who were at the front of the church praying for each other and loudly praising Him. I instantly got down on my knees and placed my forehead on the carpet when He said, "No, come sit next to me."

I sat down next to Him and He pointed toward the people and said, "Do you see that? They don't even realize you're gone." As I contemplated the implications of that statement, He told me that it made Him happy and was exactly what He wanted: everyday people praying for each other and giving *God* all the glory. He ended by saying that I was to continue doing this same thing: to go into places and start fires in people's hearts for God and go to the next place and do the same thing.

Every Christian who has ever read the "Great Commission" has been given the same instructions from Jesus. We are all called into full-time ministry. It might not be your vocation, but as a Christian it should be your lifestyle. In Matthew's description, Jesus tells us to make disciples, baptize them, and teach them (see Matt. 28:18-20). In Mark's account of the Great Commission, Jesus says that "those who believe" will do many things including casting out demons and laying hands on sick people and watching them recover (see Mark 16:15-18). When the Lord speaks to us, we need to Hear Him, understand Him, and obey in order to produce a crop.

James 1:22 says, *"Do not merely listen to the word, and so deceive yourselves. Do what it says"* (NIV).

ABOUT
BRUCE VAN NATTA

BRUCE VAN NATTA has been sent on a mission from Jesus to start fires in people's hearts for God. Since being crushed under a semi-truck and having an out-of-body experience where he witnessed the angels the Lord sent, he has gone into full-time ministry. Bruce founded Sweet Bread Ministries and now shares his gripping testimony worldwide and has been featured in several media outlets including the *700*

Club, Sid Roth, TBN, *Charisma* magazine, and *Guideposts*. He also authored the book *Saved By Angels* to share how God talks to everyday people. You can invite Bruce to speak at your church, conference, special event, or invite him to hold a workshop or seminar. Many people report being healed of all kinds of sicknesses, diseases, addictions, and emotional issues after attending one of Bruce's meetings. For more information visit sweetbreadministries.com.

BOOKS BY
BRUCE VAN NATTA

SAVED BY ANGELS

A MIRACULOUS LIFE

Notes

16

170